PRESIDENTS OF THE U.S.A.

GEORGE WASHINGTON

OUR FIRST PRESIDENT

by Ann Graham Gaines

THE CHILD'S WORLD®

PUBLISHED IN THE UNITED STATES OF AMERICA

THE CHILD'S WORLD®
1980 Lookout Drive • Mankato, MN 56003-1705
800-599-READ • www.childsworld.com

ACKNOWLEDGMENTS
The Child's World®: Mary Berendes, Publishing Director

The Creative Spark: Mary McGavic, Project Director and Page Production;
Shari Joffe, Editorial Director; Deborah Goodsite, Photo Research

The Design Lab: Kathleen Petelinsek, Design

Content Adviser: Mary V. Thompson, Research Specialist, Mount Vernon Estate
& Gardens, Mount Vernon, Virginia

PHOTOS
Cover and page 3: The Art Archive/Gift of John Hill Morgan/Museum of the
City of New York/46.1a

Interior: Alamy: 4 (The Print Collector), 10 (North Wind Picture Archives), 19
(Mary Evans Picture Library); Art Resource: 32 (detail) (Terra Foundation for
American Art, Chicago); The Bridgeman Art Library International: 9 (Collection
of the New-York Historical Society), 16 (Smithsonian Institution, Washington
DC), 26 top, 26 bottom (Collection of the New-York Historical Society); Corbis:
23 and 39, 30 (Brooklyn Museum), 31 (Francis G. Mayer); Getty Images: 21
(Stock Montage); The Granger Collection, New York: 5, 13, 20, 25, 36; iStock-
photo: 44 (Tim Fan); The Library of Congress Collection: 7 and 38, 27, 28;
The Metropolitan Museum of Art, gift of Edgar William and Bernice Chrysler
Garbisch, 1963 (63.201.2): 33 and 39; Courtesy of the Mount Vernon Ladies'
Association: 14 and 38; North Wind Picture Archives: 24 (North Wind—All
rights reserved); SuperStock, Inc.: 8, 12, 17, 34, 35, 37 (SuperStock); U.S. Air
Force photo: 45.

LIBRARY OF CONGRESS CATALOGING-IN-PUBLICATION DATA
Gaines, Ann.
  George Washington / by Ann Graham Gaines.
    p. cm. — (Presidents of the U.S.A.)
  Includes bibliographical references and index.
  ISBN 978-1-60253-030-0 (library bound : alk. paper)
  1. Washington, George, 1732–1799—Juvenile literature. 2. Presidents—United
States—Biography—Juvenile literature. [1. Washington, George, 1732–1799. 2.
Presidents.] I. Title. II. Series.

  E312.66.G256 2008
  973.4'1092—dc22
  [B]

2007042704

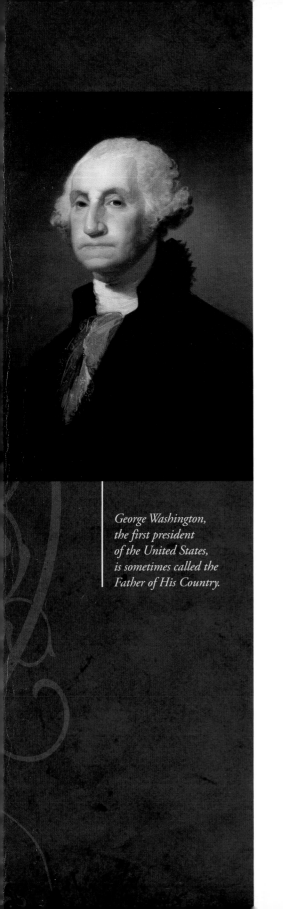

*George Washington,
the first president
of the United States,
is sometimes called the
Father of His Country.*

TABLE OF CONTENTS

CHAPTER ONE

A SOLDIER'S LIFE

Today George Washington is remembered as the first president of the United States. What most people do not know is that he was also a **surveyor,** a soldier, a farmer, and a businessman. They also do not realize that he found it difficult to be president.

George Washington was born on February 22, 1732. His father, Augustine, was a well-connected, hardworking man. He owned tobacco farms and an iron foundry in what was then the colony of Virginia. He lived there with his large family. Augustine had had four children with his first wife. After she died, Augustine married George's mother, Mary Ball. They went on to have six children. George was the oldest.

By the time George Washington was 11, his family was becoming more prosperous. They lived on Ferry Farm, along the Rappahannock River in Virginia. Like

George Washington was a military hero before he became president.

many colonists at the time, especially in the South, the Washingtons owned slaves.

Washington was a big, strong boy. He loved the outdoors and was good at playing ball. He was an excellent horseman and spent much of his time roaming his family's land. He explored the woods and streams. Sometimes he rode a ferry across the river to visit the town of Fredericksburg. As an adult, Washington would remain an adventurous outdoorsman. He also enjoyed quiet, indoor pastimes, such as listening to music, writing letters and journal entries, reading newspapers and books, and playing cards.

Although George Washington was always known for his honesty, the famous story about him chopping down his father's cherry tree—and then telling the truth about it—is a legend.

From an early age, George Washington was fascinated by his father's tools, which included an ax and surveying instruments.

People who want to teach children the value of honesty often tell a story about George Washington. In this story, he chopped down his father's cherry tree. When his father asked who did it, young Washington immediately confessed, "I can't tell a lie, Pa; you know I can't tell a lie. I did cut it with my hatchet." Actually, this story never happened. A biographer named Mason Weems made it up for a book, *The Life of George Washington,* published in 1800. What is true is that George Washington valued honesty very highly.

After Augustine Washington died in 1743, George began spending more time with his half brother Lawrence. Their father had given Lawrence a **plantation** called Mount Vernon. This lovely farm sat on the banks of the Potomac River. While living at Ferry Farm, Washington had learned his lessons from his parents and a hired tutor. He also attended a small local school. His family never had enough money to send him to college, but he would continue learning while he was with Lawrence.

Washington once went with neighbors to the Shenandoah Valley. They traveled there to make a survey, a map of land they had been granted by the King of England. On this journey, Washington realized that he loved being out in the wilderness. He also was quite good at surveying.

When Washington reached age 16, he was nearly full grown. He was a huge man for his day and stood more than six feet tall. It was time for him to start earning his own living, just like other colonists his age. He eagerly accepted a job as a surveyor. This job would send him to the far West, the land beyond the Blue Ridge Mountains. Yet even while he was working as a surveyor, he was also beginning a new career, as a soldier. Lawrence Washington belonged to Virginia's **militia,** or volunteer army. In 1751, he arranged for George to learn to use a gun and a sword so that he could join, too.

In 1752, Lawrence Washington died, to George's great sorrow. When George was just 21 years old,

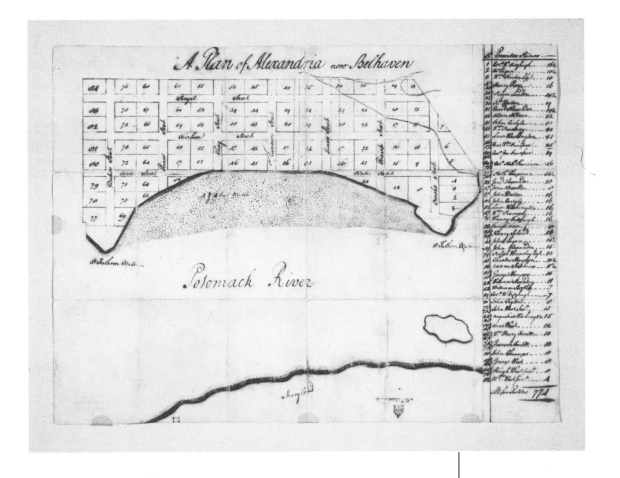

Virginia leaders asked him to carry a message to the Ohio River valley, where the king of England had given a group of Virginians a large piece of land. The problem was that the French were trying to settle there, too. Washington made his way through rain and snow to reach the French and deliver the governor's message that they should leave. The French refused to go.

Washington returned to tell Virginia leaders the bad news. The British and the American colonists decided to fight the French for these western lands. The French joined forces with their Native American **allies,** and the French and Indian War began.

George Washington was trained as a surveyor during his teenage years. He worked on at least 150 maps during his lifetime. When he was 16 years old, Washington prepared this map of Alexandria, Virginia.

Washington first showed his leadership qualities during the French and Indian War. This painting shows Captain Washington at the 1755 Battle of Monongahela.

Much of the war was fought in the wild, often in terrible, cold weather. Washington was lucky to return home unwounded and in good health. He became a hero in the French and Indian War. As commander of the entire Virginia militia, he protected many settlements on the frontier. It was then that the colonists first recognized Washington's skillful military leadership.

At the end of the war, Washington returned to Virginia, where he had begun renting Mount Vernon from his half brother Lawrence's heirs. Soon he married a widow named Martha Dandridge Custis. Martha had two young children. She was a small, motherly woman who helped George Washington enjoy his time at home. Washington still loved to be outdoors. He would always be a superb horseman who enjoyed hunting.

George Washington inherited Mount Vernon in 1761. He liked to work on his farms. He did some experimenting with plants and trees and tried to grow new crops. Martha brought more than 15,000 acres of farmland into their marriage. She also had money that they used to buy even more property. George Washington was now a rich man.

Washington's fellow colonists respected him. He was elected four times as a **representative** to Virginia's House of Burgesses. This was the group of people who made laws for the colony. He became well known for being thoughtful and thorough. He did have a temper, but he tried hard to keep it under control. George Washington cared a great deal about what other people thought of him.

Over time, the British began to tax their American colonies more and more. Many colonists, including

We do not really know what George Washington looked like as a young man, because he did not have his first portrait painted until he was 40. We know that he was very tall and had narrow shoulders.

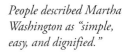

People described Martha Washington as "simple, easy, and dignified."

*The **Continental Congress** appointed Washington general of the American army. He left Virginia for Massachusetts to take command.*

George Washington took only one trip outside North America in his entire life. In 1751, he sailed to Barbados with his half-brother, Lawrence. They went there because Lawrence had a serious illness and hoped the island's tropical climate would help cure him.

Washington, began to talk of fighting back. At first, they only wanted to make England stop taxing them so much. Later, they decided the colonies should break away from Britain. "The crisis is arrived," wrote Washington, "when we must assert our rights." Virginians elected

Washington as one of the representatives to the colonies' Continental Congress.

In April of 1775, the British learned that Americans were preparing for war. The colonists had stockpiled gunpowder in Concord, Massachusetts. British soldiers marched there, planning to seize the Americans' **ammunition.** It was then that the first battles of the American **Revolution** broke out. Soon afterward, the **Continental Army** was organized. Americans considered Washington a fearless soldier and a good leader, so Congress named him general of the new army. He wrote to his wife, saying he had accepted the job: "I have used every endeavor in my power to avoid it ... but a kind of destiny ... has thrown me upon this service.... It was utterly out of my power to refuse."

Washington told Congress that he would take the assignment "at the expense of my ... ease and happiness." He refused to accept pay because he did not want to make any profit from the war. At first, Washington fought simply because he wanted the British to leave the American colonies alone. Later he believed his army was fighting for "the right of all people to govern themselves without outside interference." In other words, he believed that in their struggle for independence, the American colonies were fighting on behalf of people all over the world.

George Washington commanded the Continental Army for eight years. He proved a great commander. At times, he had to convince other Americans to keep fighting, even if it seemed they would lose. He

On Christmas night in 1776, Washington and his men boarded boats in the middle of the night. They crossed the Delaware River in the dark to reach the enemy's camp. In a surprise attack, the Americans won the Battle of Trenton. Winning this early battle helped encourage them to continue their fight for independence.

inspired his soldiers with his courage and dedication. Often, his army was at a disadvantage. They had fewer men and supplies than the enemy. Sometimes his men were cold and hungry. Washington shared his soldiers' hardships.

At the beginning of the war, Washington was victorious at the siege of Boston, but later lost to the British in New York and New Jersey. But Washington didn't give up. Finally, after a year and a half of fighting, the Continental Army won their first battle on the day after Christmas, 1776.

By 1780, the American army was again in trouble. There had been more victories, but they were running short of food, shoes, and other supplies. Finally, France joined the war to help the Americans. Together, the Americans and French were able to beat the British. On October 19, 1781, British General Cornwallis **surrendered** at Yorktown.

In one famous battle during the French and Indian War, Washington had a horse shot out from under him two times. By the battle's end, Washington had four bullet holes in his uniform, but he had not been hurt. He became known as a very brave man.

Washington and his troops spent a horrible winter encamped at Valley Forge, Pennsylvania, in 1777–78. It was bitter cold and the men were running out of food and clothing. Only the force of Washington's leadership held the troops together during this time.

MOUNT VERNON

As a grown man, George Washington lived at Mount Vernon, a huge plantation that stretched for miles along the Potomac River in Virginia. He ran five separate farms on his land.

When Washington began renting Mount Vernon from his brother's widow, the plantation had only a modest house. He started remodeling and enlarging it before his marriage. A significant addition was begun just before the American Revolution. He returned to Virginia after the war to a place run down by eight years of neglect. Still, he was thrilled to be at Mount Vernon again. "I am to become a private citizen on the banks of the Potomac," wrote Washington. "Free from the busy scenes of public life, I am retiring within myself."

Washington finished the building project he had started before the war began. He designed the grounds around the mansion to include a forest border, meadows, walkways, and orchards. Between the mansion and the shores of the Potomac River was a park, with tame deer. Eventually, Washington's home became one of the most elegant houses in the United States.

Today Mount Vernon is a national monument. Thousands of people visit George Washington's home every year. For close to two centuries, Mount Vernon changed very little. In 2006, however, a new state-of-the-art museum opened there.

CHAPTER TWO

FIRST TO LEAD

Although the American Revolution ended in 1781, Washington's army did not disband for two more years. The United States and Britain did not sign a peace **treaty** until September of 1783. Washington held his position as general until the British army left the country in November. Then he retired from his **commission** as commander of the Continental Army. He had spent eight years away from home. A grateful nation thanked him.

Washington returned to Mount Vernon. He was happy to be home, able to enjoy life on the plantation once again. He spent time with his wife, Martha. By now she had grandchildren. They enjoyed time they spent as a family. They entertained friends and neighbors. Many people came to see Washington to pay their respects. Still, both George and Martha also had many responsibilities. They owned more than 200 slaves. She ran a large household. He managed the huge plantation that stretched over 10 miles. Washington liked to visit each of Mount Vernon's five farms every day. He had 3,000 acres planted with crops, and he also raised cattle.

George and Martha
Washington loved
their days together at
Mount Vernon. They
often spent time with
Martha's grandchildren.
Many people wanted to
meet the heroic former
general, and Washington
often had guests.

George Washington
was called the Father
of His Country even
before the American
Revolution was over.
The phrase was first
used to describe him
in a 1779 newspaper.

Washington hoped this was how he would spend the rest of his life. This wish, however, would not come true. From the very beginning, the new nation faced a crisis. Even before the war ended, the 13 colonies had begun to call themselves states and formed a union. After much argument, they had approved the **Articles of Confederation** to set up a central government. Americans were afraid to give a few men too much power, however. They did not want a strong Congress to make laws that everyone had to obey. Instead, each state was responsible for its own business. Each state collected its own taxes, issued its own money, built its own roads, and so forth.

The Articles of Confederation had joined the states together. Unfortunately, it provided them with no strong central government. Washington and other leaders feared that such independent states might cause the weak Union to fall apart. They decided that the Articles of Confederation should be replaced by a **constitution.**

As a result, the Constitutional Convention was held in Philadelphia. George Washington attended as a representative of Virginia. The members of the convention met to write the U.S. Constitution. They put Washington in charge by electing him as their chairman. He did not write the Constitution, but he led the convention meetings. By nature, Washington was a friendly, quiet, polite man. But in his years as a soldier, he also had showed himself to be strong-willed, stern, and fair. Men looked up to him as a leader.

After the American Revolution, some people wanted George Washington to declare himself king.

When Washington presided over the Constitutional Convention, he helped shape the nation's most important laws—the very foundation of American government.

George Washington had to wear false teeth. He replaced them over and over again, trying to find ones that were comfortable. He never had a wooden set, but he did have some carved out of ivory.

Terrible arguments broke out between the **delegates** at the Constitutional Convention. How would the new government work? Delegates debated who should lead the government. They decided the country needed a president. It took them a long time to agree, however, how he should be elected and how long he should stay in office.

Even though he tired of the arguments, Washington realized that he and the other delegates were doing something amazing. "You will permit me to say that a greater drama is now acting on this theater than has heretofore been brought on the American stage, or any other in the world," Washington wrote in a letter. He believed it was an incredible honor for people to create their own government.

On September 17, 1787, representatives of 12 states signed the Constitution. This act turned the new nation into a **republic.** It established a federal government with three separate parts—the **executive, judicial,** and **legislative** branches. It established **checks and balances.** This made sure that no branch could have too much power. The office of president was created as part of the executive branch.

Once the convention agreed on the Constitution, voters from at least nine states had to accept it. It took a full year for this to happen. Then Americans elected a Congress, which set up an **Electoral College.** On February 4, 1789, the Electoral College voted for a president. The ballots were counted on April 6. George Washington had won by **unanimous** vote.

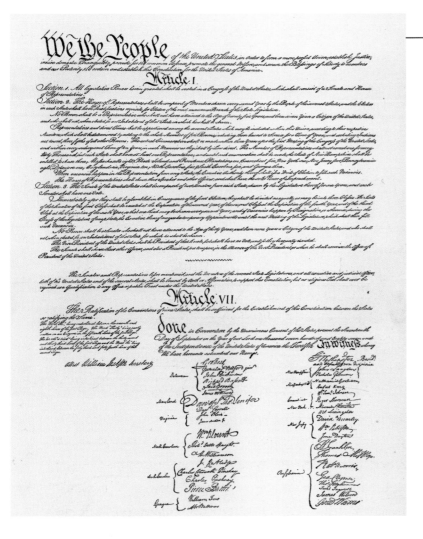

George Washington was the first person to sign the Constitution. His signature can be seen at the top of the righthand column of signatures.

George Washington was not the only man considered for the office of president. John Adams was also a possibility. He came in second, which in those days meant he became vice president.

George Washington learned that he had been elected president eight days later. He did not **campaign** for the office, and he was not interested in **politics.** In fact, he said being the president would be the "greatest sacrifice of my personal feelings and wishes."

Even though he did not want to be president, Washington accepted the position. He believed it was his duty to continue to lead his country. It still seemed

19

*Washington arrived in New York City for his 1783 **inauguration** amid much fanfare.*

possible that the Union might fall apart one day. He was determined to keep that from happening.

Becoming president meant that George Washington had to leave his plantation, trusting others to run it. He was sad, but he made the necessary arrangements. Just a few days after being elected, he left Virginia bound for New York City, where he would be sworn into office. It would be an amazing journey. All along the way, crowds turned out to greet him. He was cheered. Mothers brought their children to witness what they knew was a historic event. People seemed to feel hope that an exciting new era was about to begin.

INAUGURATION

Americans rejoiced when George Washington was elected the first president of the United States. In April of 1789, he left Mount Vernon in a carriage. He was bound for New York City on a journey that would take eight days. Washington worried that the American people might be unhappy about his election because after the Revolution, he had said he would leave public life altogether. His mind soon eased. All along the route, people turned out to cheer him. People shot off cannons and lit bonfires in his honor. When he reached the capital city of New York, he refused to get in a carriage, preferring to walk. As he went by, the people lining the streets fell silent and bowed to him.

President Washington took his oath of office on April 30. He stood outside on a balcony at Federal Hall. A huge crowd witnessed the event, and grand celebrations followed.

CHAPTER THREE
★★★★★★★★★★★★★★★★★★★★★★★

THE EXPERIMENT

After his inauguration in New York in April 1789, George Washington moved into a mansion in the heart of the city. Martha Washington and her grandchildren arrived there one month later. It took George Washington just a short time to establish a routine and get down to the business of helping establish the new government. From the beginning, he was interested in keeping in touch with the people. He wanted to find out what concerned them. So the new president met with members of the public several times a week. He had a reception for gentlemen on Tuesday afternoons and a dinner with members of Congress on Thursdays. Each Friday evening, he also went to a reception hosted by his wife. This gathering was attended by both men and women.

Twice during his first term, he took long tours of other parts of the country. In the fall of 1789, he visited Connecticut, Massachusetts, and New Hampshire. Later he visited the southern states. These trips gave him an idea of what was happening outside of New York.

During his first year as president, Washington spent most of his time getting the executive branch

George Washington went to the Senate only one time. He wanted its members to approve a treaty with the Creek Indians. When the senators wanted to go over the treaty word by word, he became very angry. After that, he never attended another meeting of Congress. Other presidents do not attend Congress, either.

up and running. When he entered office, he and John Adams, his vice president, were the only staff members in the executive branch. Congress had decided that the government should be divided into departments that would make up the rest of this branch. Washington had to choose men to head these departments, forming his **cabinet.** He appointed Thomas Jefferson as the secretary of state. The secretary of state

Washington is shown (at far right) with three members of his cabinet (left to right): Henry Knox, Thomas Jefferson, and Alexander Hamilton. Washington was determined not to choose friends, family, or the wealthy for his cabinet, but rather men who he felt had the greatest reputations in the country.

is in charge of U.S. relations with other countries. As secretary of the treasury, Alexander Hamilton took care of the nation's **finances.** Washington named Edmund Randolph as the attorney general, the person in charge of the country's legal matters. Henry Knox was the secretary of war. He was responsible for the military. Washington also chose another 350 men to fill other, less important jobs.

The new government had a huge job. It had to develop relations with other countries, including

England, Spain, and France, all of whom claimed lands bordering the United States. There was trouble in the west with Native Americans, who were concerned about the westward expansion of the United States. In addition to these problems, the government also needed money. Washington hoped, too, for the government to have time to take care of smaller matters, like setting up a post office and establishing rules concerning how new immigrants could become citizens.

During Washington's first term, his life was threatened by two different illnesses. Both times, rumors spread that he was dying. Americans were distraught. In one case he had developed a tumor on his leg, which had to be removed by a surgeon. This was a very painful procedure in those days. But the president recovered quickly and went back to work.

President Washington's government established the Bank of the United States to help pay the states' debts from the Revolutionary War.

Slowly, progress was made. One of the first achievements of the government was the establishment of the National Bank. It took over the huge debts some states had acquired, fighting the Revolution. It also collected taxes and issued currency.

In one way, this represented a victory for George Washington, who would always work hard to make sure that the states helped each other out. Yet talking about how to deal with financial problems led to disagreements between the nation's leaders about what the nature of the government should be. In particular, Secretary of the Treasury Alexander Hamilton got into very heated arguments with the Secretary of State Thomas Jefferson. Hamilton wanted there to be a strong central government. Jefferson wanted to make sure states' rights would always be protected. Their disagreements would eventually result in the formation of **political parties.**

Other achievements during Washington's first term included Congress's decision about where to locate the new national capital. In 1791, the capital was moved to Philadelphia. But this was just a temporary location. The government had decided that a new city should be built to serve as the seat of the

Two of Washington's most important advisors were Thomas Jefferson (top) and Alexander Hamilton (bottom).

Capitol, 38: 53. N.
Long. 0: 0.
GEORGE TOWN
PLAN
of the CITY of
Washington
in the Territory of Columbia,
ceded by the States of
VIRGINIA and MARYLAND
to the
United States of America,
and by them established as the
SEAT of their GOVERNMENT,
after the Year
MDCCC.
President's House
Capitol
PART OF VIRGINIA WITHIN THE TERRITORY OF COLUMBIA.
POTOMAK RIVER.
EASTERN BRANCH
PART OF MARYLAND WITHIN THE TERRITORY OF COLUMBIA.
OBSERVATIONS
explanatory of the
Plan.
Breadth of the Streets.
THE grand Avenues, and such Streets as lead immediately to public places, are from 130 to 160 feet wide, and may be conveniently divided into foot ways, walks of trees, and a carriage way. The other Streets are from 90 to 110 feet wide.
IN order to execute this plan, Mr. ELLICOTT drew a true Meridional line by celestial observation, which passes through the Area intended for the Capitol; this line he crossed by another due East and West, which passes through the same Area. These lines were accurately measured, and made the basis on which the whole plan was executed. He ran all the lines by a Transit Instrument, and determined the Acute Angles by actual measurement, and left nothing to the uncertainty of the Compass.
SCALE OF POLES.

Washington chose the location for the new nation's capital city. It was a plot of land on the Potomac River that covered about 10 square miles. He asked a famous French architect named Pierre L'Enfant to design the city.

federal government. Following George Washington's suggestion, a site on the Potomac River was selected. This would become the city of Washington, D.C. Also during this time, the court system was set up, and the Constitution was amended for the first time, when Congress added the Bill of Rights.

During his first term, George Washington set some important **precedents** that would affect how the

*Washington helped oversee the design of the new U.S. Capitol building. It originally housed not only both branches of the Congress but also the **Supreme Court** and the Library of Congress.*

United States government works. He did not attend regular sessions of Congress. He gave Vice President Adams little to do. He decided to use his **veto** power only if Congress passed a law that he believed was **unconstitutional.** He never refused to sign a bill into law because of his personal feelings about it. Some later presidents would use their veto power differently, vetoing laws simply because they believed they were bad ideas. The nation's court system was also set up during Washington's first term. After the Supreme Court was established, it took the responsibility for deciding whether a law was unconstitutional.

For a long time, Washington did not intend to run for a second term. He wanted to go home. He had also been hurt by some people's criticism of his formal manners. He thought it was important to create respect for the office of the president. To do so, he had attendants open doors and introduce him. He held many formal receptions. Some said he acted too much like a king. The American president was supposed to do things more simply.

Washington was also bothered by people saying that he had wanted the new capital built near his home so that it would bring money into that part of Virginia. Washington considered this an attack on his integrity. He also did not like the fact that two political parties were beginning to form, under the leadership of Thomas Jefferson and Alexander Hamilton.

The election of February 1793 drew near. It seemed that most Americans still wanted Washington to be president, even if some people criticized him. Unlike later presidents, Washington was not a member of a political party. He was not nominated by a group such as the Democrats or the Republicans. Instead, an individual nominated him for the office. Washington longed to return to Mount Vernon. But he did not remove his name from the list of **candidates** and he was unanimously elected president for a second time.

George Washington understood very well that he was setting an example for other presidents to follow. He proved it when he said, "I walk on untrodden ground. There is scarcely any part of my conduct which may not hereafter be drawn into precedent."

FIRST LADY MARTHA WASHINGTON

Martha Washington was not happy when her husband was elected president. But she knew that he felt obligated to serve, so she decided to do all she could to help him. Martha was by nature a warm and lively woman, whose life revolved around her family. She liked life at Mount Vernon best. Nevertheless, she moved to New York City to live with her husband soon after he was inaugurated. During her trip there, she was treated much as he had been—towns rang their bells to announce her arrival and crowds gathered to see her.

Like many women of her time, Martha Washington had not been very well educated. She did, however, have plenty of experience helping her husband manage their plantation. She had also traveled throughout the country to be with her husband. She spent almost half of the American Revolution in his military camp, where she was often one of the few women there. As the wife of the president, she drew on these experiences. She helped him entertain very important diplomats and ordinary people at receptions and dinners. It's interesting to note that Martha Washington was not called the First Lady. This was a term that would not be invented for more than sixty years.

CHAPTER FOUR

A SECOND TERM

George Washington was inaugurated for the second time in 1793. His second term as president was even harder than his first.

During Washington's second term, he had to pay a great deal of attention to relations with other countries and with America's native peoples. Native Americans threatened settlers in the West. George Washington tried to make peace with them. He wanted to protect the Indians' rights to own land. He also wanted to keep them from siding with enemies of the United States, as they had done in the French and Indian War.

At that time, Europe was in an uproar. Revolution had broken out in France. Its new government declared war on Britain. The United States needed to maintain peaceful relations with France and Britain. Washington believed the best thing for the United States was not to side with one country or another.

Noted American artist Gilbert Stuart painted many portraits of George Washington, including this one from the late 1790s.

George Washington is the only president who never lived in the White House. Although construction on the White House began in 1792, it wasn't ready to be lived in until 1800, when John Adams was president.

With the signing of Pinckney's Treaty, the United States gained access to the Mississippi River, an important trade route. This famous painting by George Caleb Bingham shows workers on a flatboat along the Mississippi in the 1800s.

He wanted the United States to remain **neutral.** Many Americans disagreed with him over this issue, but in the long run he had his way.

One of Washington's great successes during his second term was to force some European powers to leave parts of the North American continent. To help accomplish this, he sent Supreme Court Justice John Jay to Britain. Jay got the British to agree to give up its forts in the Northwest Territory. In exchange, the United States repaid debts it owed to Britain. The treaty helped increase trade between Americans and the British, which helped the American economy. Pinckney's Treaty, signed between the United States and Spain, gave Florida and land along the Mississippi River to the United States. It also allowed Americans to use their boats on the Mississippi. Now the United States could use the river to transport both people and goods across the continent and to the sea.

At home, an important event was the Whiskey Rebellion. Congress had passed a tax on whiskey. People living in western Pennsylvania threatened to revolt because they did not want to pay this tax. Washington ordered the rebels "to retire peaceably to their homes." When they refused, he called out thousands of militia soldiers. He rode west to meet his new army. They settled the matter without bloodshed. Washington's actions showed American citizens that the states had to obey laws passed by the United States government.

In 1796, the American people wanted Washington to run for a third term, but he refused. He was beginning to feel old and wanted to retire. John Adams won the election and became the new president. In his farewell address, Washington told the nation his hopes and dreams for its future: "I shall carry to my grave the hope that your Union and brotherly affection may be perpetual; that the Constitution may be sacredly

In his farewell address, George Washington told Americans that he thought it was a very bad idea to create political parties.

Construction began on the Washington Monument in 1848, but the project was not completed for nearly 40 years. The Civil War and lack of funding halted its construction. When it was finally finished in 1884, the monument stood more than 555 feet (169.2 meters) tall, making it the tallest building in the world at the time.

Washington owned 80,000 acres of land at the end of his life.

maintained; and that free government ... the ever favorite object of my heart ... will be the happy reward of our mutual cares, labors and danger."

George and Martha Washington went home to Mount Vernon to lead a happy, quiet life. Washington spent his time tending his farms and animals. Managing such a vast plantation took much of his energy.

One day, Washington rode out on a snowy day to inspect his farms and came down with a cold. He stayed close to home the next day, but went outside for a little while to mark some trees he wanted to cut down. That evening he was a little bit hoarse. Very early the next day, before dawn, he woke his wife to tell her he was having trouble breathing, but he would not let her call the servants or the doctor. By the time the sun rose, Washington was very sick with a severe throat infection. He died late at night, on December 14, 1799. He was 67 years old.

Americans felt tremendous sorrow when they learned Washington had died. Congressman Henry Lee honored Washington as he spoke before Congress: "To the memory of the Man, first in war, first in peace, and first in the hearts of his countrymen."

Both the capital city and a state were named in George Washington's honor. In 1848, construction of the world-famous Washington Monument began. It would pay respect to both the first president and to the nation's capital. The monument stands as a towering reminder of Washington's enormous contributions to his country. The dollar bill and the quarter both bear his image. Schools, streets, bridges, and parks are named for Washington as well.

An entire nation continues to honor the man that many feel to be the greatest American president of all. Few understand how hard it was for him to fill that office.

Washington always regretted that he and Martha did not have any children.

The faces of four great presidents—George Washington, Thomas Jefferson, Theodore Roosevelt, and Abraham Lincoln—are carved into the side of Mount Rushmore in South Dakota. Artist Gutzon Borglum oversaw the massive project, which began in 1927 and took 14 years to complete.

SLAVERY

George Washington lived in a world in which slavery was accepted. When he was a child, his father owned slaves. As an adult, Washington inherited some slaves and bought others. The number of slaves at Mount Vernon also grew because Washington's slaves married and had children. Although Virginia law did not allow slaves to marry, Washington did recognize unions between husband and wife.

Still, Washington sometimes treated his slaves in a way that seems cruel today. For example, he sold a rebellious slave and used the profits to buy rum and food. Slaves worked from sun up until sun down, six days a week. Today many people cannot understand how a man who valued liberty and freedom ever could have owned slaves at all.

George and Martha Washington depended on slaves to work in the house and on the farms of Mount Vernon. Just before the Revolution, however, George Washington decided that he would no longer sell slaves without their consent. Although he stood by his word, his decision hurt him. As more slaves bore children and he switched to crops that required fewer people to harvest them, he had to support more people than he needed. At one point, he had more than 300 slaves at Mount Vernon.

As he grew older, Washington felt more and more strongly that slavery was wrong, although he never pushed publicly for its end. Many Americans still believed in slavery at the time. If Washington had spoken out against it, he might never have been elected president. In 1793, Washington decided his goal would be to free all of his slaves, but he had not figured out how the ex-slaves could support themselves. He realized his family would have to support the children and the people who had become too old to work. He hoped neighboring farmers might be willing to hire the rest.

After Washington left the presidency in 1797, he continued to think about ways to free the slaves at Mount Vernon. In the summer of 1799, he wrote his will. It arranged to free all the enslaved people on the plantation who belonged to him, or about half the total number, upon Mrs. Washington's death. It had not been possible for Washington to free the others, because they belonged to the heirs of Mrs. Washington's first husband.

1730	1740	1750	1760	1770

1732
On February 22, George Washington is born in Westmoreland County in Virginia. His father, Augustine Washington, is a tobacco farmer and businessman. Mary Ball Washington, George's mother, is Augustine's second wife.

1743
Augustine Washington dies. After his death, 11-year-old George Washington begins spending more time at his half brother Lawrence's home, called Mount Vernon.

1748
Still a teenager, George Washington goes along with his neighbors when they travel to the wild Shenandoah Valley to make a map of a large tract of land they had been granted by the king of England.

1749
Washington is appointed surveyor for Culpeper County, Virginia.

1751
George Washington sails to the Caribbean island of Barbados with Lawrence. It is the only time he will ever leave North America.

1753–1754
Washington is sent west by the governor of Virginia to order the French to leave British lands in the Ohio country. Soon the French and Indian War breaks out, in which Washington plays a prominent part. He begins renting Mount Vernon from Lawrence's widow.

1755
Washington takes part in an expedition against the French under the leadership of British General Edward Braddock. He is lucky to escape with his life and gains a reputation as an excellent soldier.

1759
After being elected to the Virginia House of Burgesses and leaving the army, George Washington returns to his plantation and marries Martha Dandridge Custis, a young widow with two children.

1761
George Washington inherits Mount Vernon.

1774
The colonists grow increasingly angry about Britain's taxation. They form the Continental Congress to unite and decide what to do. George Washington is elected to represent Virginia as a delegate to the First Continental Congress. At that time, few colonists are interested in independence from Britain.

1775
On April 19, the battles of Lexington and Concord take place, and the Revolution begins. Washington is appointed a member of the Second Continental Congress. On June 15, Congress appoints him commander of the colonists' Continental Army. Washington goes to Boston to take command.

1776

The British leave Boston. The Continental Congress signs the Declaration of Independence on July 4, formally declaring the American colonies' independence from Britain. France begins to secretly send weapons and money to the Americans. On Christmas night, George Washington and his soldiers cross the Delaware River in the middle of the night to surprise the enemy in what will be known as the Battle of Trenton, a badly needed American victory.

1777

After wins at Brandywine Creek and Germantown, Washington and his army suffer through a long, cold winter at Valley Forge.

1778

France joins the Revolution on the side of the patriots, and the tide begins to turn in favor of the Americans.

1781

After the Battle of Yorktown, British General Cornwallis surrenders on October 19. This ends the American Revolution.

1783

British troops leave the continent in November, more than two years after their surrender. American soldiers complain that they still have not received the promised pay for their time in the military. Washington secures a promise from Congress that the soldiers who fought in the Revolution will receive the pay they are owed. Washington resigns his commission as commander in chief and is finally able to go home. He is delighted to return to Mount Vernon.

1786

Many Americans express dissatisfaction with the Articles of Confederation. Washington corresponds with other leaders to decide what should be done.

1787

Leaders decide to create a constitution to replace the Articles of Confederation. Washington is elected president of the Constitutional Convention, which takes place from May to September. In the fall, delegates sign the Constitution and send it to be accepted by the states.

1789

On February 4, Washington is elected the first president of the United States. He is inaugurated in New York City, the nation's capital city, on April 30. He selects the first presidential cabinet.

1790

Congress selects a permanent place for the U.S. capital city, a site along the Potomac River suggested by President Washington.

1792

Washington is reelected as president.

1794

The Whiskey Rebellion breaks out when farmers in Pennsylvania pick up arms in protest of a tax the government has placed on alcohol. George Washington rides to Pennsylvania to assume control of the American army but then resolves the conflict without bloodshed. In Jay's Treaty, Britain gives up its posts in the Northwest Territory, a region that will become a number of Midwestern states.

1795

Pinckney's Treaty opens the Mississippi River to American boats, allowing the transport of goods and people up and down the river.

1796

In the fall, newspapers throughout the country publish Washington's Farewell Address, which let the nation know he would not be a candidate for a third term.

1797

President Washington's second term comes to an end. John Adams, Washington's vice president, becomes the second president of the United States.

1799

On December 14, Washington dies at Mount Vernon. The nation mourns his death.

39

allies (AL-lize) Allies are nations that have agreed to help each other, for example, by fighting together against a common enemy. The United States and France were allies during the American Revolution.

ammunition (am-yuh-NISH-en) Ammunition is bullets, cannonballs, and other things that can be exploded or fired from guns. Americans began to stockpile ammunition before the Revolution began.

Articles of Confederation (AR-teh-kelz OF kun-fed-uh-RAY-shun) The Articles of Confederation made up the first plan for a central U.S. government. Under the Articles of Confederation, there was no strong national leader, only a Congress.

cabinet (KAB-eh-net) A cabinet is the group of people who advise a president. George Washington appointed his cabinet soon after he became president.

campaign (kam-PAYN) If people campaign, they take part in activities, such as giving speeches, in the hope of winning an election. George Washington did not campaign to become the president of the United States.

candidates (KAN-deh-dats) Candidates are people who are running in an election. Several candidates run for president every four years.

checks and balances (CHEKS AND BAL-en-sez) Checks and balances are the limits the Constitution places on the branches of the federal government. For example, the president is commander-in-chief of the army, but only Congress can declare a war. Checks and balances prevent any one branch from becoming too powerful.

commission (kuh-MISH-en) A commission is a position of power that is given to a person by the government or another authority. George Washington received a commission to become the commander of the Continental Army.

constitution (kon-stih-TOO-shun) A constitution is the set of basic principles that govern a state, country, or society. The U.S. Constitution describes the way the United States is governed.

Continental Army (kon-tuh-NEN-tul AR-mee) The Continental Army was the American army that fought in the American Revolution. George Washington was the commander of the Continental Army.

Continental Congress (kon-tuh-NEN-tul KONG-gris) The Continental Congress was the group of men who governed the United States during and after the Revolution. George Washington was a member of the first and second Continental Congress.

delegates (DEL-uh-gitz) Delegates are people who are elected by others to take part in something. Each colony sent delegates to the Continental Congress.

Electoral College (ee-LEKT-uh-rul KOL-ij) The Electoral College is made up of representatives from each state who vote for candidates in presidential elections. Members of the Electoral College cast their votes based on what most people in their state want.

executive (eg-ZEK-yuh-tiv) An executive manages things or makes decisions. The executive branch of the U.S. government includes the president and the cabinet members.

finances (FYE-nan-siz) Finances are the money and income that a person, country, or company has. The secretary of the treasury is in charge of the nation's finances.

inauguration (ih-naw-gyuh-RAY-shun) An inauguration is the ceremony that takes place when a new president begins a term of office. George Washington's first inauguration was in New York City.

judicial (joo-DISH-ul) Judicial means relating to courts of law. The judicial branch of the U.S. government includes its courts and judges.

legislative (LEJ-uh-slay-tiv) Legislative means having to do with the making of laws. The legislative branch of the U.S. government is Congress, and Congress makes the nation's laws.

militia (muh-LISH-uh) A militia is a volunteer army, made up of citizens who have trained as soldiers. Virginia and other colonies had militias for times of emergency.

neutral (NOO-trul) If a country is neutral, it does not take sides. George Washington believed the United States should remain neutral, rather than take sides in European wars.

plantation (plan-TAY-shun) A plantation is a large farm or group of farms. Mount Vernon was the name of George Washington's plantation.

political party (puh-LIT-uh-kul PAR-tee) A political party is a group of people who share similar ideas about how to run a government. Today the two major U.S. political parties are the Democratic and Republican parties.

politics (PAWL-uh-tiks) Politics refers to the actions and practices of the government. George Washington did not have a natural interest in politics.

precedents (PRES-uh-dentz) Precedents are actions that later serve as examples for others to follow. When presidents purposely try to act as George Washington would have, they follow his precedents.

representative (rep-ree-ZEN-tuh-tiv) A representative is someone who attends a meeting, having agreed to speak or act for others. Congress is made up of representatives elected by the American people.

republic (ree-PUB-lik) A republic is a nation in which citizens elect representatives to their central government. The United States became a republic after the Constitution was approved.

revolution (rev-uh-LOO-shun) A revolution is something that causes a complete change in government. The American Revolution was a war fought between the United States and England.

Supreme Court (suh-PREEM KORT) The Supreme Court is the most powerful court in the United States. The Supreme Court decides if laws are unconstitutional.

surrender (suh-REN-dur) If an army surrenders, it gives up to the enemy. When British General Cornwallis surrendered, he promised his soldiers would no longer fight against the Americans.

surveyor (sur-VAY-ur) A surveyor is a person who determines the boundaries of a piece of land. Surveyors used to make maps of a property while they measured it.

treaty (TREE-tee) A treaty is a formal agreement made between nations. The United States and England signed a peace treaty after the American Revolution ended.

unanimous (yoo-NAN-uh-mess) If something is unanimous, everybody agrees on it. Because every member of the Electoral College voted for George Washington, their vote was unanimous.

unconstitutional (un-kon-stih-TOO-shuh-nul) If something is unconstitutional, it goes against the Constitution of the United States. The Supreme Court decides whether laws are unconstitutional.

veto (VEE-toh) A veto is the president's power to refuse to sign a bill into law. Unless a large majority in Congress votes to overrule the veto, the bill does not become law.

THE UNITED STATES GOVERNMENT

The United States government is divided into three equal branches: the executive, the legislative, and the judicial. This division helps prevent abuses of power because each branch has to answer to the other two. No one branch can become too powerful.

EXECUTIVE BRANCH

PRESIDENT
VICE PRESIDENT
DEPARTMENTS

The job of the executive branch is to enforce the laws. It is headed by the president, who serves as the spokesperson for the United States around the world. The president signs bills into law and appoints important officials such as federal judges. He or she is also the commander in chief of the U.S. military. The president is assisted by the vice president, who takes over if the president dies or cannot carry out the duties of the office.

The executive branch also includes various departments, each focused on a specific topic. They include the Defense Department, the Justice Department, and the Agriculture Department. The department heads, along with other officials such as the vice president, serve as the president's closest advisers, called the cabinet.

LEGISLATIVE BRANCH

CONGRESS
Senate and
House of Representatives

The job of the legislative branch is to make the laws. It consists of Congress, which is divided into two parts: the Senate and the House of Representatives. The Senate has 100 members, and the House of Representatives has 435 members. Each state has two senators. The number of representatives a state has varies depending on the state's population.

Besides making laws, Congress also passes budgets and enacts taxes. In addition, it is responsible for declaring war, maintaining the military, and regulating trade with other countries.

JUDICIAL BRANCH

SUPREME COURT
COURTS OF APPEALS
DISTRICT COURTS

The job of the judicial branch is to interpret the laws. It consists of the nation's federal courts. Trials are held in district courts. During trials, judges must decide what laws mean and how they apply. Courts of appeals review the decisions made in district courts.

The nation's highest court is the Supreme Court. If someone disagrees with a court of appeals ruling, he or she can ask the Supreme Court to review it. The Supreme Court may refuse. The Supreme Court makes sure that decisions and laws do not violate the Constitution.

CHOOSING
THE PRESIDENT

It may seem odd, but American voters don't elect the president directly. Instead, the president is chosen using what is called the Electoral College.

Each state gets as many votes in the Electoral College as its combined total of senators and representatives in Congress. For example, Iowa has two senators and five representatives, so it gets seven electoral votes. Although the District of Columbia does not have any voting members in Congress, it gets three electoral votes. Usually, the candidate who wins the most votes in any given state receives all of that state's electoral votes.

To become president, a candidate must get more than half of the Electoral College votes. There are a total of 538 votes in the Electoral College, so a candidate needs 270 votes to win. If nobody receives 270 Electoral College votes, the House of Representatives chooses the president.

With the Electoral College system, the person who receives the most votes nationwide does not always receive the most electoral votes. This happened most recently in 2000, when Al Gore received half a million more national votes than George W. Bush. Bush became president because he had more Electoral College votes.

THE WHITE HOUSE

The White House is the official home of the president of the United States. It is located at 1600 Pennsylvania Avenue NW in Washington, D.C. In 1792, a contest was held to select the architect who would design the president's home. James Hoban won. Construction took eight years.

The first president, George Washington, never lived in the White House. The second president, John Adams, moved into the house in 1800, though the inside was not yet complete. During the War of 1812, British soldiers burned down much of the White House. It was rebuilt several years later.

The White House was changed through the years. Porches were added, and President Theodore Roosevelt added the West Wing. President William Taft changed the shape of the presidential office, making it into the famous Oval Office. While Harry Truman was president, the old house was discovered to be structurally weak. All the walls were reinforced with steel, and the rooms were rebuilt.

Today, the White House has 132 rooms (including 35 bathrooms), 28 fireplaces, and 3 elevators. It takes 570 gallons of paint to cover the outside of the six-story building. The White House provides the president with many ways to relax. It includes a putting green, a jogging track, a swimming pool, a tennis court, and beautifully landscaped gardens. The White House also has a movie theater, a billiard room, and a one-lane bowling alley.

PRESIDENTIAL PERKS

The job of president of the United States is challenging. It is probably one of the most stressful jobs in the world. Because of this, presidents are paid well, though not nearly as well as the leaders of large corporations. In 2007, the president earned $400,000 a year. Presidents also receive extra benefits that make the demanding job a little more appealing.

★ **Camp David:** In the 1940s, President Franklin D. Roosevelt chose this heavily wooded spot in the mountains of Maryland to be the presidential retreat, where presidents can relax. Even though it is a retreat, world business is conducted there. Most famously, President Jimmy Carter met with Middle Eastern leaders at Camp David in 1978. The result was a peace agreement between Israel and Egypt.

★ *Air Force One*: The president flies on a jet called *Air Force One*. It is a Boeing 747-200B that has been modified to meet the president's needs.

Air Force One is the size of a large home. It is equipped with a dining room, sleeping quarters, a conference room, and office space. It also has two kitchens that can provide food for up to 50 people.

★ **The Secret Service:** While not the most glamorous of the president's perks, the Secret Service is one of the most important. The Secret Service is a group of highly trained agents who protect the president and the president's family.

★ **ThePresidential State Car:** The presidential limousine is a stretch Cadillac DTS.

It has been armored to protect the president in case of attack. Inside the plush car are a foldaway desk, an entertainment center, and a communications console.

★ **The Food:** The White House has five chefs who will make any food the president wants. The White House also has an extensive wine collection.

★ **Retirement:** A former president receives a pension, or retirement pay, of just under $180,000 a year. Former presidents also receive Secret Service protection for the rest of their lives.

F A C T S

QUALIFICATIONS

To run for president, a candidate must

* be at least 35 years old
* be a citizen who was born in the United States
* have lived in the United States for 14 years

TERM OF OFFICE

A president's term of office is four years.
No president can stay in office for more than two terms.

ELECTION DATE

The presidential election takes place every four years on the first Tuesday of November.

INAUGURATION DATE

Presidents are inaugurated on January 20.

OATH OF OFFICE

I do solemnly swear I will faithfully execute the office of the President of the United States and will to the best of my ability preserve, protect, and defend the Constitution of the United States.

WRITE A LETTER TO THE PRESIDENT

One of the best things about being a U.S. citizen is that Americans get to participate in their government. They can speak out if they feel government leaders aren't doing their jobs. They can also praise leaders who are going the extra mile. Do you have something you'd like the president to do? Should the president worry more about the environment and encourage people to recycle? Should the government spend more money on our schools? You can write a letter to the president to say how you feel!

1600 Pennsylvania Avenue
Washington, D.C. 20500
You can even send an e-mail to: president@whitehouse.gov

Books

Adler, David A. *George Washington: An Illustrated Biography*. New York: Holiday House, 2004.

Davis, Kenneth C. *Don't Know Much About George Washington*. New York: Scholastic, 2004.

Rosenburg, John. *First in Peace: George Washington, the Constitution, and the Presidency*. Brookfield, CT: Millbrook Press, 1998.

Schanzer, Rosalyn. *George vs. George: The Revolutionary War as Seen by Both Sides*. New York: National Geographic, 2004.

Videos

The American President. DVD, VHS (Alexandria, VA: PBS Home Video, 2000).

Biography: George Washington, American Revolutionary DVD (New York, A & E Home Video, 2004).

The History Channel Presents The Presidents. DVD (New York: A & E Home Video, 2005).

The History Channel Presents Washington the Warrior. DVD (New York: A & E Home Video, 2006).

The Life of George Washington. VHS, DVD (Whittier, CA: Finley-Holiday Film Corp., 2005).

National Geographic's Inside the White House. DVD (Washington, D.C.: National Geographic Video, 2003).

Internet Sites

Visit our Web page for lots of links about George Washington and other U.S. presidents:

http://www.childsworld.com/links

Note to Parents, Teachers, and Librarians: We routinely verify our Web links to make sure they are safe, active sites—so encourage your readers to check them out!

INDEX